N-E-T-WORKING
<u>N</u>ow <u>E</u>verything <u>t</u>he <u>Working</u> Public Needs to Know

Published by
American Book Business Press™
An imprint of American Book Publishing
5442 So. 900 East, #146
Salt Lake City, UT 84117-7204
www.american-book.com

Printed in the United States of America on acid-free paper.

N-E-T-Working: Now Everything the Working Public Needs to Know

Designed by Troy D. O'Brien, design@american-book.com

Publisher's Note: *This publication is designed to provide accurate and authoritative information in regard to the subject matter covered. It is sold or distributed with the understanding that the publisher and author is not engaged in rendering legal, accounting, or other professional service. If legal advice or other expert assistance is required, the services of a competent professional person in a consultation capacity should be sought.*

ISBN-13: 978-1-58982-423-2
ISBN-10: 1-58982-423-7

Library of Congress Cataloging-in-Publication Data

Zabora, Theodore J.
N-E-T-Working, now everything the working public needs to know : a step-by-step, time-tested, and proven strategy to find your new job / Theodore J. Zabora.
    p. cm.
Includes bibliographical references and index.
ISBN-13: 978-1-58982-423-2
ISBN-10: 1-58982-423-7
1. Job hunting. 2. Business networks. I. Title.

HF5382.7.Z33 2007
650.14--dc22

2007020959

Special Sales

These books are available at special discounts for bulk purchases. Special editions, including personalized covers, excerpts of existing books, and corporate imprints, can be created in large quantities for special needs. For more information e-mail info@american-book.com.

N-E-T-WORKING
Now Everything the Working Public Needs to Know

A Step-by-Step, Time-Tested, and Proven Strategy to Find
Your New Job

THEODORE J. ZABORA

Dedication

To Nancy, my wife and best friend

Table of Contents

Part One

Part Two

Part One

Introduction

So you want to network? Before we begin, it is important for you to understand right up front that organization, hard work, perseverance, and discipline are required for a successful search.

Perhaps you're familiar with the term *networking* or you've heard about the process, but you're not sure how to effectively do it. This book outlines a step-by-step process that will help you find the job opportunity you want. The strategy has never failed me.

If you were laid off, you may begin the networking process feeling anxious and worried. Perhaps you are coping with the uncertainty of your future, which makes it difficult to focus.

The termination package you received may not be adequate. Severance, benefit continuation, and outplacement support services are insufficient. You now need a job as quickly as possible in order to meet financial and personal goals or family responsibilities.

If you are currently employed, maybe you don't respect your boss. He or she doesn't treat you with respect or value your perspective, contributions, and experience. The company doesn't support training and development, and you may feel that you aren't reaching your full potential.

If you are a recent college grad, you are probably asking questions like, where do I begin, or who do I contact. You may have started applying to advertised positions or have received career counseling, but networking is the *best* approach to finding a new job. There is an opportunity for you to feel motivated, productive, and professionally satisfied, and this book is the road map.

I have experienced all of the emotions and challenges of trying to find a job that met my personal goals and needs. That's why I decided to write this book.

My simple goal is to outline a process, which has been extremely successful for me, tested over twenty-five years. What better way to use my experiences than to help you find the job you've always wanted?

During the networking process, it is critical for you to understand that you will experience many ups and downs, and your emotions will face many challenges. Obviously, this is not an easy process. Persevere. Have faith that your networking efforts will be rewarded.

At times you will be excited because several organizations will react favorably to your résumé or application. At other times, you will feel frustrated because the same organizations put the position on hold, decided to promote from within, or perhaps you were the company's second choice and did not receive an offer. Therefore, I encourage you to always remember one thing. "DON'T GIVE UP! DON'T EVER GIVE UP" (more in Step Nine).

Many professionals have contacted me over the years as part of their networking process. I asked them, "How many networking contacts have you made?" They respond by saying, "Ted, I have been extremely busy networking. I know I'm doing all the right things. I'm happy with where I am and what I have been doing. To answer your question, I would say I have made almost thirty-five contacts in the last three months. That's pretty good, right?"

Before I respond, I say to myself, thirty-five? You can make thirty-five contacts in a couple of hours, in a morning, let alone in three months. You need to have a structured and disciplined approach.

Networking, without question, is a numbers game. Over the last twenty-five years, I have kept the following statistics and noticed the following trends.

Let's say you make two thousand networking contacts. Only ten percent or two hundred will respond. Doesn't sound good? Only two hundred out of two thousand. Don't be discouraged by any means.

Of the two hundred contacts, only seventy percent, or 140, may know of a potential opportunity for you to pursue. And, of the 140 contacts, typically twenty percent, or twenty-eight, are viable positions. That means that two thousand contacts equal twenty-eight excellent opportunities.

Think about that. Twenty-eight opportunities. Incredible! Your efforts will be rewarded.

Three thousand contacts could potentially identify forty-two viable opportunities. That kind of activity will certainly keep you motivated and focused. You will be rewarded for your efforts.

Keep in mind that these opportunities don't include the positions you apply to because the majority of positions identified through networking are not advertised. It is, without question, a numbers game. The more contacts you make, the more opportunities you'll find. Please do not forget that.

In my experience, the most contacts I've ever had to make were 3,300. During that process, seventy-two companies contacted me to conduct a telephone screening, schedule an interview, or clarify my salary expectations. I received an offer six months after my last day of work and after only three months of severance. The position was well worth the wait.

The least number of contacts that I've made is four hundred, which resulted in an offer after two months of being unemployed. Timing, organization, hard work, perseverance, and discipline are everything.

There is one myth about the networking process that I need to mention. Many professionals emphasize how critical it is to meet personally with people, "press the flesh" as they say.

While it is important from time to time, in my opinion it is not absolutely critical to the networking process. Some people will want to help you but don't have the time. Many people, however, will ask you to keep in contact and let them know how you are doing with your search. If they want to meet, they will extend an invitation.

This book was written to help you. If only one individual is successful in his or her networking, the book will be a success.

One last thought. Networking is a challenge, but it works. Try not to get discouraged. Best wishes.

I would be happy to hear and learn about your networking experiences. Please write to me at:

Ted Zabora
P.O. Box 73
Baldwin, MD 21013

Now let's look at the nine-step process.

Step One:
Identify Networking Sources

Are you are an NFL football fan? Whether you are or not, "Are you ready for some networking?" LET'S GO!

Welcome to a nine-step process that has proven successful over twenty-five years. It is a time-tested strategy that will help you find that new job.

Remember hard work, perseverance, discipline, and organization are required for a successful job search. If you develop those habits, your efforts will be rewarded.

The layoff will become a distant memory, or you will transition to a new company that is more in-line with your values, goals, and objectives. As a recent college grad or soon-to-be grad, you may identify the best possible opportunity. Let's begin.

Step One requires you to identify every possible source for your job search. This is critical because you will identify all of your potential networking opportunities. The positions found through networking are usually not advertised, so determining your contacts will open up opportunities that you wouldn't have been aware of.

Take fifteen minutes to think about and make your list of contacts and sources. Your goal is to come up with ten. I will help you. The first source is friends. Only nine more to go. **Do not read the next paragraph until you have finished your list.**

Now, let's compare. I would use the following sources: relatives, friends, neighbors, professional membership directories, peers, professional associations, internet searches, professional meetings, chambers of commerce, business and economic development directories, business organizations, websites, and college or graduate alumni sources. The key in Step One is to identify as many contacts as you can. Were you able to come up with other sources?

Did you have questions about professional associations as a key source? Not sure who they are? Simply do an internet search such as *professional engineering associations* to identify excellent sources. Here are some examples:

HUMAN RESOURCES:
- Society for Human Resources Management (SHRM)
- Identify your state's local HR chapter

INFORMATION TECHNOLOGY:
- Association of Information Technology Professionals (AITP)

- Information Technology Professionals Association (ITPA)

NEW COLLEGE GRADUATES:
- Do a web search for *career development* and *job search advice for new college graduates*
  (You will find many sites to use including www.IMdiversity.com, www.WorkTree.com, and www.jobsonline.net. Remember. They are just one source in your effort to identify as many sources as possible in Step One of the process.)

ENGINEERING:
- Society of Women Engineers (SWE)
- American Academy for Environmental Engineers (AAEE)

ACCOUNTING:
- American Accounting Association
- American Institute of Certified Professional Accountants (AICPA)

The majority of these sources will list their contact information (email addresses, telephone numbers, and voicemail numbers). The identification of the sources makes you fully prepared for Step Two in the nine-step process.

While many of the sources are self-explanatory, there are two examples that need further discussion. The purpose is to demonstrate how creative you can become.

Several years ago I was networking for a senior human resources opportunity. I knew the corporate officers of

Maryland companies would be excellent contacts. I did an internet search for *Maryland Company Corporate Officers*. The result was extensive email and telephone contact information for me to use as networking sources.

Another example is exploring professional associations. If they have the capability to exchange email, it can be an outstanding and powerful source to network.

In my case, I sent an email with my résumé. By clicking on *send,* seven hundred professionals instantly knew I was networking for a senior HR opportunity. Check with the association to explore this capability.

Now let's talk specifically about a mechanical engineer, an English major, and an HR generalist. Each of them contacted me as part of their networking efforts. The mechanical engineer was laid off from his company after twenty-three years of service. He was obviously very concerned and frustrated, as any professional with a family would be.

He had applied to newspaper and website opportunities only. Until we discussed the nine-step process, he was unaware of what networking was and how effective it could be. After making six hundred contacts, he became employed within a relatively short period of time. After seven months, he was able to match his former salary of $85,000 a year.

Another excellent example is the English major I agreed to meet. He was disappointed with the progress of finding an opportunity after relocating to Maryland from the west.

Although he seemed overwhelmed at first, he began to understand the methodology. The more contacts you make, the more likely it is to find that new job. He, too, was successful with his search. He was pleased with a starting salary of $45,000. After gaining several years of additional editing experience, he was able to move to another company in a higher level position and starting salary of $70,000.

Lastly, an HR generalist was frustrated with his search until he realized and understood the point that the more contacts you make, the more likely it is you will identify an opportunity. He, too, found a new position recruiting for a financial organization. He matched his former salary of $40,000 within three months.

Here are three excellent illustrations of why you should never assume, and that contacts can be found in places where you may least expect it. First, I knew an experienced human resources professional. He had spent all of his time contacting vice presidents and directors of human resources for his search. He excluded lower level HR professionals (generalists, specialists, and administrative support) from his networking process.

He assumed his next-door neighbor, who was a secretary, could not help him. He told me, "How would she know of a senior human resources opportunity?"

After talking to me, he contacted her. Neighbors are one of many sources we identified in Step One.

Her company was looking for a director of HR. He applied and ultimately received an offer. NEVER ASSUME.

Second, I was having my hair cut. My barber knew I worked in human resources. He had another customer whose wife had recently lost her job. He gave my number to this woman, and she contacted me. I was able to give her several leads. NEVER ASSUME.

Third, there was an individual who was on my staff. For a number of reasons, he and I decided it was best for his career to begin networking for a new position.

I offered my assistance by giving him several contacts. He interviewed and received an excellent offer from a well-known, outstanding company. He was well respected and worked for them for over twenty years.

However, he was never in touch with or aware of the local job market. He was pleased with the company and his career, and he wasn't concerned about keeping his options open.

But, since a critical step in the nine-step process is NEVER ASSUME, I would contact him periodically as part of my networking. Although I contacted him three or four different times, he was never able to assist me.

I wanted to look for a more satisfying professional opportunity. Fortunately, I stepped back and said to myself, "Never Assume." I contacted him, and he said, "You are not going to believe this. I just received a letter from an executive recruiting firm in Florida. They are doing a search for the division of a major steel producer in Baltimore. The job description describes you perfectly."

I contacted the recruiter, interviewed, and accepted an offer. NEVER ASSUME.

STEP ONE TIME-TESTED LESSONS:

- Identify every source possible to assist you with you search.

- Brainstorm and be creative.

- Ensure you take full advantage of professional associations.

- Remember timing, hard work, perseverance, discipline, and organization.

- Never assume a contact or source may not be able to help you.

- Remember the engineer, English major, HR generalist, neighbor, my barber, and my staff member.

Ready for Step Two?

Step Two:
Develop a Script

In today's interactive, instant-communication world, most individuals have email and voicemail. This makes it simple for you to make the hundreds of contacts required for a successful search. Meeting with someone in person is certainly helpful, but it is not absolutely necessary. This is significant because you can communicate with individuals whom you have never met, but who may be able to help you with your search.

In Step Two, you should develop a script to use when contacting each of your new sources from Step One. It should be tailored to your specific background, experience, and education. This script serves as a powerful summary that is a snapshot of your abilities and experience. Spend the necessary time to formulate your script. This is a first impression that could make a great difference in your career.

When constructing your script, be brief but to the point. Each contact is busy with his or her individual responsibilities, company challenges, and objectives, so you want to not only make a good impression, but you want to make a memorable impression. Just like the initial review of your résumé, your email or voicemail will only get a couple minutes of attention.

If they want more information about you and your background, they will contact you. For example, they may know about an opportunity but want to know your salary expectations. Are you flexible with relocation? What is the maximum distance for your daily commute? If you are a manager, would you be interested in an individual contributor role? Have you retained your certifications? Is a lateral move of interest if there is potential for growth?

The following example is a time-tested, thirty-second script (again, brief but very specific) which can be used for email and voicemail. In the email I have always attached my résumé.

> (*Contact's name*), this is Ted Zabora. I am currently Vice President of Human Resources for ABC Corporation. I am contacting you because I am networking to identify a senior human resources position for myself. I wanted to see if you might know of an opportunity for me to explore.
>
> My educational background includes a bachelor's degree in psychology and a master's degree in human resource management. I have extensive experience both as a

generalist and specialist at the corporate and division levels in a variety of for-profit industries—union and nonunion.

If you are not aware of an opportunity now, I would sincerely appreciate if you could keep me in mind. My phone number is _____. Thank you.

NOTE: If you are currently employed, you should make the following change: "The reason for my *confidential contact* is that I am networking to identify a senior human resources position for myself." You do not want to jeopardize your current position.

If you are using email for your search, here is a word of caution. More and more companies are monitoring email use. They may also stipulate that email is for business only. Unless you have the permission of your current company, you will want to obtain a home email account.

Here is another script example that might be helpful:

(Contact's name), my name is Betty Becker. I am currently a help desk administrator for XYZ Corporation. I am contacting you because I am networking to identify a similar position for myself, hopefully with the opportunity for growth and development. I wanted to see if you might know of an opportunity for me to explore.

My educational background includes a bachelor's degree in information systems and a minor in business administration from the University of Maryland, Baltimore County. I am also HDI and MicrosoftMCDST certified.

If you are not aware of an opportunity now, I would sincerely appreciate if you could keep me in mind.

My phone number is _____. Thank you.

Remember that when you are developing your thirty-second script, you should include the following:
- Your current position
- The objective of your search
- Educational background
- Experience summary
- Professional accomplishments

Create a script that, like your résumé, will leave a lasting impression. And don't be discouraged if only 10 percent of the contacts respond (remember the statistics in the introduction). Keep pushing forward and don't give up.

STEP TWO TIME-TESTED LESSONS:

- Develop a concise summary of your background and experience.

- Develop a voicemail or email that the contact can listen to or read in thirty seconds.

- Attach your résumé to the email.

- Do not be overly concerned about getting a personal introduction. You will be able to make a thousand contacts in two months.

- Mention confidentiality if you are currently employed.

- Do not jeopardize you current position.

On to Step Three.

Step Three:
Maintain Contact Lists

In Part Two, B and C, you will find ten forms. You can make additional copies to ensure your search is organized. Remember, to successfully network, you must be organized. Getting organized will help you accomplish the following:

- Monitor your search activity
- Follow up with your contacts
- Plan your next strategy
- List the method of contact
- Identify trends
- Provide structure
- Ensure discipline

Organization will also enable you to maintain the name of the contact, date of contact, how you contacted them (email, voicemail, in-person), and the outcome—if further action is required.

For example, the contact could ask you to send them your résumé and follow up in two weeks. Or, they may be aware of a developing opportunity and ask you to follow up in a month.

You may now be asking, "Ted, how many contacts should I make per week?" I worked for a company that was not a match for my values and did not provide a great deal of professional satisfaction. It was not unusual to work sixty hours or more per week and also make twenty-five contacts in the evening. Therefore, what is a good networking number each week? Guess before looking at the next paragraph.

The number is 125. How surprised were you? After working six days a week, taking Sunday off to rest, you will have made six hundred contacts in a month and three thousand within five months. Timing is everything.

If you were laid off, this number is not unrealistic at all. If you are working but unhappy with your present company, you will have to have a disciplined and structured regiment to meet the goal. Remember. It is a numbers game.

You also need to retain your contact lists. You never know when your company will begin to face serious financial challenges or bring in a new manager who does not share your values. Perhaps you will develop concerns about the organization which were not present when you accepted the position.

Here is a perfect example. Two years after contacting one of my sources, I was re-contacted by that individual. My résumé described what her client was looking for in terms of skills, abilities, and experience. She wanted to know my employment status. After looking through my notes, I saw that this contact was a very professional individual.

Since my current company had missed significant financial targets, I aggressively pursued the opportunity. Maintain your contact lists because you never know when they will be needed again.

STEP THREE TIME-TESTED LESSONS:

- Use the forms to organize and structure your search.

- Continue to focus on the other requirements: hard work, perseverance, and discipline.

- Follow up with your contacts at the appropriate time.

- Make 125 contacts a week.

- Take Sunday off. After a long week, it is important to set aside some relaxation time.

- Maintain the contact lists as possible sources in the future. You never know what it will bring. There are no guarantees in life.

- Review your lists and notes two months into your search. How close are you to making one thousand contacts?

Let's go to Step Four.

Step Four:
Send a Thank-You

Every individual in Step One who responds to your contact should receive a thank-you. Not only is it the appropriate thing to do, it is common courtesy. However, many people do not do it.

Saying thank you takes so little time but is so significant. An individual will remember you regardless if they knew of an opportunity or not. Even if the contact is not aware of any opportunities right now, still send them a thank-you. It only takes a few minutes to respond to their communication. Do not underestimate its power.

I cannot tell you how many times I have heard, "No one ever responds to my voicemails or emails." Remember the person who contacted me two years after my original contact?

I had sent her an appropriate thank-you which helped me to develop a lasting networking contact.

Email and voicemail messages are very effective. It does not necessarily have to be a handwritten note. However, a handwritten note is also appropriate if you do not have email and voicemail contact information. You can always call your contact's company for his or her position title and address.

Depending on the communication you receive, appropriate responses are:

- Thank you. If you could continue to keep me in mind, I would sincerely appreciate it.
- Thank you very much. Please contact me if you need any additional information about my background and experience.
- Thank you. As you suggested, I will contact you in a month (or whatever timeframe the contact suggested).
- Thank you. I will keep you informed.

If you make the commitment to keep a contact informed, do it. You never know the impact of your actions and the impression you will form.

Over the years, I have heard significant feedback and acknowledgment from my networking contacts of a thank-you even though they were not aware of an opportunity.

Again, the contact took the time to respond to you. You will be remembered because you took the time to simply say thank you.

STEP FOUR TIME-TESTED LESSONS:

- Send an appropriate thank-you, which can make a significant impact on the individual contacted.

- Send an email, leave a voicemail, or write a handwritten note to the contacts who respond to your networking search.

- Send a thank-you to every company that responds to your résumé or application.

- Take the little time to say thank you for a potential reward, short-term and long-term.

- Extend courtesy and professionalism, which will make an impression on the contact.

- Follow up on every commitment you make.

Ready for Step Five?

Step Five:
Apply to Advertised Positions

Simultaneously and in conjunction with Step Three, begin to apply for opportunities that you find. Newspapers are obviously only one source. Make sure you access websites (monster.com, careerbuilder.com, 6figures.com, hotjobs.com, simplyhired.com, GadBall.com, and CareerLadder.com to name a few).

In addition, you should use professional association journals and newsletters as well as the alumni office of your alma mater. As you did in Step One, identify every source possible in order to identify position opportunities.

As discussed in Step Four, I would also send a thank-you to every company who responds to your résumé or application. While you may not be a match for the current opportunity, you never know what needs may develop in the future.

As you apply to positions, do not assume you are over- or under-qualified. Why? Because the company may not receive the response they had hoped for. You may meet seventy percent of the requirements. In addition, the company may realize what you bring to them and restructure the position.

Many individuals I have met over the last twenty-five years used the sources listed in Step Five. They became extremely frustrated and often said, "Ted, it's like my résumé goes into a black hole never to be seen again."

You cannot use these sources alone for your search because many positions are never advertised. If you sit and wait to respond until you have an advertised position that is perfect for you and meets all your professional and personal goals, your search will likely be extremely long. Why? Because most positions are not advertised. NETWORK!

Let's say you respond to a newspaper or website opportunity. You know you want to be aggressive and show the company your interest. However, when do you follow up? Many people think, "If I follow up on a regular basis, they will think I am aggressive. Right?" The answer is no.

After the company receives your résumé or application, wait three weeks, then follow up with them to determine the potential status of the position and the organization's level of interest.

Wait an additional three or four weeks. Follow up again. At that point seven weeks will have elapsed, and you will know if the company is interested or not. You may not be happy with the answer, but two contacts are sufficient for you to demonstrate your aggressiveness and interest in the opportunity.

One last point. Don't be surprised if the company contacts you three or four months down the road. This is not as crazy as it sounds.

Many companies and HR professionals get turned off if you follow up and contact them frequently. In my recruitment experience, I communicated upfront in the process. Depending on the opportunity, I would say, "The response to our opportunity has been overwhelming. I will contact you if there is interest in your background. Thank you for your interest in our company, and best wishes with your search."

Even after this communication, there have been candidates who contacted me every other day for two weeks. Why? Because he or she was desperate.

Using the three and seven week rules will not create a turnoff. In addition, it may result in a contact at a later date. You can wait to demonstrate your aggressiveness during the interview process.

STEP FIVE TIME-TESTED LESSONS:

- Supplement your networking efforts by applying to advertised positions.

- Use many sources to identify positions of interest such as the newspaper, web postings, and professional publications.

- Do not assume you are overqualified or under-qualified unless it is obvious. Bottom line. The only thing you are risking is a stamp or an email.

- Increase the success of your search because the advertised position may have been filled, but the contact may know of another opportunity for you to explore.

- Do not turn off the company by being too aggressive.

- "Follow up" is not synonymous with "aggressiveness."

- Do not apply to advertised positions alone. NETWORK.

Let's go to Step Six.

Step Six:
Follow Up with Contacts

By this time you have organized your search by maintaining contact lists. Here is another one of Ted's rules.

After identifying and contacting one thousand contacts in Step One (approximately two or three months), begin to contact them *again*. This step is critical because an excellent opportunity may now be available.

Why? They might not have known about an opportunity two or three months ago, but now they could help. Or they may have misplaced your résumé or contact information. TIMING IS EVERYTHING.

Do not assume they would have contacted you if they were aware of an opportunity. I once contacted a company four months after the position was first available. They had put the position on hold to address several unforeseen business issues. I then scheduled an interview.

At this point in your search, verify that you have been making 125 contacts a week. Remember, it's a numbers game.

You can use a similar script to the one you developed in Step Two. Just modify it.

(Contact's name), my name is _____. I contacted you _____ months ago. I was networking for a _____ opportunity. I just wanted to follow up to see if you might know of an opportunity now. If not, please continue to keep me in mind.

If you do not have my contact information and résumé, may I forward them to you again? My phone number is _____.

Thank you. I appreciate your time and help.

In the networking process, timing is everything. It is all about who you contact and when you contact them. If you eliminate the contact all together because they weren't able to help you, you are possibly missing out on a potential opportunity in the future. Following up is just as important as the initial contact.

STEP SIX TIME-TESTED LESSONS:

- Do not assume the contacts in Step One would have contacted you if they knew of an opportunity.

- Understand individuals are busy and may have misplaced your contact information.

- Modify your original voicemail or email when you follow up.

- Follow-up provides another means of structure for your networking search.

- Remember that timing is everything.

On to Step Seven.

Step Seven:
Never Assume

Never assume an individual will be unable to assist you with your job search. That is a terrible mistake. Also, never assume an organization will not have interest or renewed interest in your background.

I worked for a company whose division was closing. Since I was going to be there until the end, I was able, with the company's knowledge, to do some networking.

Compensation experience is a significant part of my background. I saw an advertised opportunity for a senior compensation analyst. However, I had been a manager and director. My first reaction was that the salary wouldn't meet my expectations. NEVER ASSUME?

I decided it was worth a stamp, and I applied to the position. What I did not know is that the head of the function wanted to bring somebody in as an analyst and within six months promote them to a manager. I interviewed and accepted an offer. The promotion and compensation package were excellent.

As I've mentioned before, never assume that the company you are working for will be around forever or that you will be with that company for a long time. I accepted an opportunity with a medical center. I was enthused about the opportunity of becoming a key member of the senior HR team. Prior to accepting the position, I had networked and interviewed for several other excellent opportunities.

The VP of HR, to whom I reported, was out placed after I had been there for only a month. He was the consummate HR professional, and politics played a role in his dismissal. He had an outstanding senior HR reputation. I respected him totally.

The action told me a lot about the organization. My first thought was to contact the other opportunities I had considered. But I was worried that they wouldn't be interested in me since I only worked at the center for a month.

I had interviewed with a manufacturing company. The vice president/general manager was receptive when I described the circumstances. I interviewed with thirteen individuals and accepted an offer.

It was the most challenging and rewarding HR position I had at that point in my career. NEVER ASSUME.

In another situation, I was working for a large business services company. I decided to leave the company due to significant differences with the new senior VP of HR regarding philosophy, style, and values.

I heard that a local bank had been searching for an individual with my background. Most of my networking contacts communicated that there must be a problem because the position has been vacant for a long time.

My first reaction? Don't touch this opportunity with a hundred-foot pole. NEVER ASSUME?

I decided to contact the bank, and I learned why the position was vacant so long. I interviewed and accepted the offer on New Year's Eve, even though the holidays are usually a slow time for employment offers. It was an excellent opportunity. NEVER ASSUME.

Do not automatically assume an organization will not be interested in your background if you lack specific industry experience.

Assuming the following is true, the key points to communicate are:

- I am flexible.
- I learn quickly.
- I am adaptable to change.
- I can develop credibility within a relatively short period of time.
- I bring other perspectives to the organization.
- I have the skills, background, and experiences needed to impact and contribute to the organization.

At one point in my career, I had assumed that receiving a negative reference was a major issue. I learned this was not true. If you have an excellent background, have a positive interview, and receive excellent feedback, I believe you can overcome a poor reference.

Things are so different in 2007 than they were twenty or thirty years ago. If you are truthful and explain what happened, it may not be as significant as you thought. If it is significant to the company, the organization is probably not worth joining.

Never assuming plays a major role in networking. As mentioned in previous chapters, you must never assume that an individual can't help you with your job search. (Remember my neighbor, the secretary, and my barber from Step One?) But you should also never assume that a company wouldn't be interested in you or that you won't be interested in a certain company. Be open to a variety of opportunities.

STEP SEVEN TIME-TESTED LESSONS:

- Never assume an individual cannot help you.

- Never assume a company will not have interest or renewed interest in your background.

- Remember my personal experiences and important lessons.

- Remember an opportunity or company may not be as bad as you have heard.

Ready for Step Eight?

Step Eight:
Follow Up, Again

It is my hope you will not need Step Eight. At this point, you may be six months into your search, but remember organization, hard work, perseverance and discipline. DON'T GIVE UP. DON'T EVER GIVE UP! Do not be intimidated or shy with your second follow-up.

When you get to the end of your networking list, you may have made two thousand or more contacts. Step Eight requires you to start with your first contact, again. It is no different than Step Six, but your activity has been more extensive at this point. Your search could be at the six-month timeframe. Use a script as you did in Step Six.

Modify your script by initially stating how long it has been since your last contact. This important step keeps you in the mind of the contact. At this point, they may now know of a company planning for expansion. There may be an opportunity in the near future.

This happened to me twice. In one case, I learned a major company was relocating to the area. In the other case, I learned that a company's human resources director was not relocating to Maryland.

A good barometer is still one month of searching for each $10,000 of base salary. Therefore, a $60,000 position could take six months. A $120,000 position could take a year. This is not unrealistic.

There are exceptions to this rule. The nine-step process for me has challenged the typical timeframe.

My step-by-step, time-tested strategy to reduce the amount of time it takes to find that new job has never failed me.

When used within my process, Step Eight may be the very action that identifies the opportunity you have been searching for. Don't be shy about starting over with your contact list. You can't expect that prefect job to just fall in your lap. It takes hard work and discipline. And Step Eight will help you stay on track with your networking goals.

STEP EIGHT TIME-TESTED LESSONS:

- Follow up, again, because it may be the very step, which identifies the opportunity you have been searching for.

- Never assume the contact originally contacted will not know of an opportunity now, which is potentially six months since the start of your search.

- Modify your email and voicemail communications by stating how long it has been since you last contacted the individual.

- Don't be intimidated or shy.

Step Nine:
Don't Ever Give Up

Don't ever give up. EASIER SAID THAN DONE? I share your pain. I have been where you are, and I understand. It is not easy. However, try to focus on the long-term results. Your hard work will be rewarded.

DON'T GIVE UP. DON'T EVER GIVE UP! We face many challenges in life. The situation you are in is one of them.

Networking requires hard work, perseverance, discipline, and organization. These skills are necessary for your search to be successful.

Jimmy Valvano, former North Carolina State men's basketball coach, was an inspiration to me. In 1993, Coach V was awarded the ESPY Award given for individual and team accomplishments. His acceptance speech was incredibly moving and had a great influence on my life. His message also has significance to the networking process. The challenge and incredible depth of his message is so vital to your success. Not just to your search but to life. Jimmy said a really good day would be "if you laughed, cried, and hugged." Think about those words. They are so vital for us to put things in perspective. Life truly is a journey.

I mentioned in the Introduction that you will have many ups and downs during the networking process. As Coach V said in his speech, "DON'T GIVE UP. DON'T EVER GIVE UP!"

When things get very difficult, use your family and professional support system, make sure you are following the nine steps, and remember Coach V's words. They will provide motivation and reinforcement to ensure you are on the right path.

STEP NINE TIME-TESTED LESSONS:

- DON'T EVER GIVE UP!

- Meet and overcome another of life's challenges.

- Remember, networking requires hard work, perseverance, discipline, and organization.

- Use your support system.

- Think about Coach V's challenge to never give up. You will weather the storm.

Conclusion

It is my hope this step-by-step process will provide a structured road map for you to follow. As I mentioned before, your successful effort to find a new job will make that layoff a distant memory. You will be in a position where you feel productive, motivated, and happy. Stay focused. Your efforts will be rewarded.

If your search stagnates, review the time-tested lessons at the end of each chapter. Remember, I care about you, or I would not have written this book. It was intended to help you. Your support system cares, and I care, which will help you to NEVER GIVE UP.

In the questions and answers section in Part Two, E, I provide guidance and recommendations on many issues that may surface during the recruitment process. I have included relevant situations that will be helpful in dealing with these sometimes difficult situations and decisions.

You now have a nine-step process to effectively network. You may be early or late in your career. The steps apply to everyone. And remember, it has been time tested for twenty-five years and has never failed me.

Part Two

A
The Nine-Step Networking Process

Don't ever give up
Follow up, again
Never assume
Follow up with contacts, again
Apply to advertised positions
Send a thank-you
Maintain contact lists
Develop a script
Identify networking sources

B
Networking Contact Lists

DATE:

CONTACT:

METHOD:

OUTCOME:

SPECIFIC ACTION REQUIRED:

DATE:

CONTACT:

METHOD:

OUTCOME:

SPECIFIC ACTION REQUIRED:

DATE:

CONTACT:

METHOD:

OUTCOME:

SPECIFIC ACTION REQUIRED:

C
Potential Opportunities

POSITION:

COMPANY:

SALARY RANGE:

CONTACT INFORMATION:

ACTION REQUIRED/STATUS:

POSITION:

COMPANY:

SALARY RANGE:

CONTACT INFORMATION:

ACTION REQUIRED/STATUS:

POSITION:

COMPANY:

SALARY RANGE:

CONTACT INFORMATION:

ACTION REQUIRED/STATUS:

D
Résumé Guidelines

The purpose of this section is to give you specific guidelines for developing a well-written résumé. Your résumé will only be briefly reviewed by the employer, so it must accomplish two things for the company. First, it must show that you are a definite candidate for the position you are seeking. Second, it must clearly and accurately show the employer your background and skills.

In general, do the following:

- Focus. Remember, your résumé is the first impression the employer will form of you. It must be well written.

- Do not misrepresent your background. This could likely come back to haunt you. In most cases, the application you complete states that you can be terminated if you misrepresent yourself or lie about your background.

- Develop several résumés in order to tailor your background, skills, and abilities to the opportunity you are applying for. This does not mean you are misrepresenting your experience. It simply means you are communicating why specific aspects of your background match the position requirements.

- Ensure it is formatted well and that it is attractive for the reader to review. Use spell check.

- Include a summary of your overall experience (see my résumé in Part Two, F).

- Have a well-defined employment or professional objective.

- Include major career accomplishments.

- Use strong action verbs to highlight your career accomplishments

- Use numbers, percentages, revenue, payroll, budget, etc. to validate and highlight your accomplishments and the impact you have had on the organization

- List your exact dates of employment. Most employers want to see them. However, I have never had an issue with writing "2004 to 2005" versus "7/5/04 to 12/31/05." The exact dates are usually recorded or requested as part of the formal application process.

- If you are a very experienced candidate, specific dates for obtaining your bachelor's or master's degrees are not necessary in my opinion. If you obtained your bachelor's degree in 1969, you are probably fifty-nine or sixty years old. You want to emphasize your background, experiences, and accomplishments.

- Remember, a well-written résumé will prompt the company to call you for a phone screening or to schedule an interview. From my experience as an interviewer, these were the two key tests.

- Remember, many individuals and sources have specific insights and perspectives about what constitutes a well-written résumé.

- Reexamine your résumé if you feel you are not getting the response you had hoped for; especially if the position requirements described you perfectly.

- Make sure you will be able to explain any gaps in your employment history.

- Include your home telephone number or email address if you are concerned about contact at your current employment. You do not want to jeopardize your current position. You may not be happy with your present organization, but you want to conduct your search on your terms.

- Ask someone who can provide constructive and objective feedback to review your résumé.

- Slick résumés do not impact the interviewer. This is based on my experience and discussions with my peers. A slick résumé may include pictures, videotapes, and DVDs. It may be appropriate to include such things for a marketing or graphic design position but not for a help desk administrator, human resources generalist, customer service manager, or senior programmer. (If your picture looks like your license, you may NEVER get the interview anyway. Obviously, I am kidding.)

- As a goal, keep your résumé to no more than two or three pages at the most. Remember, the initial review of your résumé will be brief. Use white, off-white, or light beige paper and black ink. Gaudy and flashy résumés should be avoided.

E
Questions and Answers

These questions and answers will take you step by step through the recruitment, interview, selection, offer, and transition processes. The answers are based on thirty-five years of professional experience.

Good luck and best wishes for that interview to result in an offer.

RECRUITMENT:

I have applied for an opportunity. When should I follow up?

I would follow up three to four weeks after the company received your résumé or application. The human resources department does not want you to contact them every other day. You will turn them off. Aggressiveness in this area usually isn't successful in my experience.

When you contact the employer after three or four weeks, I would make reference to when they received your résumé. Tell them you would like to know the status of the opportunity and if there is interest in your background.

If you receive no communication, I would follow up again in an additional three weeks. It would have been about seven weeks since the company first received your materials.

Again, I would express my continued interest in the opportunity and ask them to please contact you to schedule an interview.

If you still do not receive any communication, I would assume there is no interest. Perhaps they are not a good fit for you if they will not respond to your communication. Move on. PERSEVERE. DON'T EVER GIVE UP.

The company is not identified in its newspaper or internet job posting. Should I apply to a blind ad?

I would, but I know individuals who would not. I know individuals who applied to their own company. I also know companies who disguised the position in such a way that the person unintentionally applied to their own position.

The downside to not applying is that you may have missed a fantastic opportunity. The company simply did not want to address all the telephone inquiries and follow-up calls.

The bottom line is that you have nothing to lose. If you apply to a company that you don't want to work for, you are under no obligation to continuing interviewing with the company.

If the company requests a cover letter, do I write one?

I typically have not done so. However, my advice would be to write one if it is requested. They may want to assess your communication skills, but more importantly they want to know why you feel you are a match for the position.

If the company requests my salary requirements, do I respond with a specific range?

I have not responded other than to say salary is negotiable. You do not want to exclude yourself until you know more about the organization, growth potential within the company, and possibly an above-average benefit package.

However, more and more companies are asking candidates to define a salary range or expectation in order to be considered for the position. Let me give you an example.

If your current salary was $50,000, I would respond by saying that your salary expectations are $50,000 to $60,000. You can always negotiate. For example, you may be eligible for a merit increase in three to six months.

REMEMBER ONE THING. The purpose of the interview is to receive an offer. It does *not* mean you have to accept.

If the company requests references before or for the first interview, should I provide them?

Yes. But I would never request references unless I was down to the final candidates. Usually they won't ask for references until after the interview, but if they ask, I would provide what is being requested.

Be careful, however. Will the references maintain your confidentiality? If you are currently employed, you want to make sure your search remains confidential and on your terms.

Should I post my résumé on a website?

For years I had never found this to be productive for me. NEVER ASSUME? All of us must be willing to continue learning.

However, more recently, I decided I should not assume. As a result, I received many calls from professional recruiters or companies who had seen my posted résumé. Several of those opportunities were excellent.

INTERVIEW:

What are your thoughts about the interview process?

I have learned over many years that you can learn a lot about your boss and the organization through the interview process.

Let's assume you receive an offer. If you experienced major communication issues during the interview process such as problems with timely feedback, the status of the position, or follow-up to your additional questions, you should probably be prepared to experience communication problems during your employment.

There is a significant correlation between how you are treated during the interview and how you are treated as an employee. I had a final interview with a company. The CEO communicated that an offer would be extended in a week. Eight weeks later there was still no communication from the executive recruiter—not a positive sign about the senior management and the type of leaders I would be working for.

Another example is when I assumed a human resources position for a medium-sized company. During the interview process, my future boss clearly demonstrated arrogance.

What happened? He was arrogant and abrasive when I became a member of his team.

You should try to learn as much as you can about the company and the employer during the interview process. If something doesn't seem right, you shouldn't accept an offer.

I have applied for an opportunity. The organization has contacted me to schedule an interview. How should I prepare for the interview?

Learn as much as you can about the company and the individual to whom you will report. You want to assure them that you are a match for the position. Asking business-related questions will demonstrate your interest in the opportunity.

Culture, values, management style, and financial stability are critical to show that you are an excellent match. Be on time, dress professionally, and bring several copies of your résumé.

During the first interview, should I ask about the benefit programs?

I would not ask unless the interviewer outlines them. If they are interested in hiring you, there will likely be a second interview. You can use that opportunity to ask for a summary of the benefits package or answers to your specific questions and concerns.

As a result of the interview, I feel I need to clarify portions of the discussion. How do I do this?

Follow up and clarify the information. If you are a strong candidate, it will enhance the process. A phone call or letter is appropriate.

What if I feel I am a perfect match for the position, but I don't think the interview went well?

Contact the interviewer and explain why you may not have performed well during the interview. You may have had a death in the family and were not at your best. You may have been anxious and nervous. You know you can contribute and have a significant impact on the organization. Hopefully, the interviewer will understand.

I know there is significant interest in my background. However, I do not feel it is a match.

Be honest and tell them why. You never know if there is information they will be able to clarify.

I have a poor reference. Should I be concerned?

I have seen candidates with outstanding references turn out to be mediocre performers. Likewise, I have seen a candidate with a poor reference turn out to be an outstanding performer.

Why? It may have nothing to do with the applicant's competence or performance. There are politics, insecure managers, personality and philosophical differences, or unfair treatment. As a human resources professional, I would not screen out a candidate based on a poor reference. However, not everyone agrees with me.

Have you ever terminated an interview in the first thirty minutes?

Yes. Why waste your time and the interviewer's? During the interview, I realized the position would never work for me. I told him politely we were not a match and thanked him for his time.

Would you bring up salary in the first interview?

68

Unless you know what it is (you are probably not going to the interview in the first place if it is too low), I would ask the company's recruiting range at the end of the interview.

If there is a long time between the first interview and second, is that a sign of no interest?

Usually it is. If you have not heard anything three weeks after the first interview, that is usually not positive.

SELECTION AND OFFER:

I am not sure the opportunity is the best for me. Have you ever turned down an offer simply because you were following your gut instinct?

Absolutely. You need to do two things. First, ask more questions or have the employer address your concerns. This may help you resolve your discomfort.

Second, follow your gut. It is usually right.

As a new or recent college graduate, I was not completely happy with the position offered. It was not exactly what I wanted. Should I accept?

This can happen frequently. If it is an excellent company with a competitive benefit program, you should seriously consider the offer.

You have the opportunity to show the organization your skills and abilities. Your disappointment could lead to increased responsibilities or potential growth in the company. You may not get you dream job right out of college. However, it will strengthen your résumé and experience.

What is the best approach to a salary offer?

Assuming the organization knows your current salary, you want to communicate that you would expect an offer based on what other employees in the same or similar positions are paid. You do not want to jeopardize the offer.

What happens if I am disappointed with the salary offer?

Ask if there is any flexibility with the salary offer. If not, check to see in the company has a six-month performance-based increase.

If my current employer makes me a counteroffer so I will not leave, should I accept?

Usually no. Typically the counteroffer has nothing to do with pay. You decided to explore other opportunities for many reasons. You may have had concerns about the environment, lack of a commitment to training and development, your boss, values, or promotional opportunities. Therefore, accepting a counteroffer will be a temporary satisfier. You may receive a salary increase, but the other concerns will remain unresolved.

You are also likely to develop resentment against the company if the issue was exclusively based on pay, and you had to interview with another company in order for your current employer to finally respond to your concerns.

What is the most appropriate way to turn down an offer?

You need to be totally professional. You want to communicate that you appreciated their time and their interest in your background. Explain to them that overall, you felt that another opportunity was a better match for you at this point in your career, and wish them continued success.

More importantly, you may want to apply to the company in the future.

The recruiting range was $50,000 to $55,000. After four interviews, I received an offer of $45,000. Should I accept?

I would not. There should not be this significant surprise at this part in the process. It would send me warning signs about the organization. Remember, I believe there is a correlation between what occurs during the interview process and your experience as a candidate.

What happens if I agree to a start date, and at the "eleventh hour" I'm contacted by another organization that is offering a better opportunity than the one I accepted?

You should tell the other organization you are extremely interested in the opportunity, but you recently accepted a position with a different company.

You need to determine how interested the company is and what their timeframe is. If you are the only candidate, that is one thing. If they are early in the process, you need to compare the risks with the opportunity you have already accepted.

If you turn down the accepted offer now, there is no guarantee you will have good chemistry with the other manager.

My experience has been that if you turn down the offer after already accepting the job, you can probably forget about working for that organization over the next several years. However, you do have to consider what is best for your career and family. Not an easy decision.

TRANSITION:

I have been incredibly frustrated with my employer. I want to quit immediately. Do I have to give two weeks notice?

Believe me, I know how you feel. I have wanted to do the same thing.

As difficult as it is, be professional and comply with the company's termination notice policy. Many times it is tied directly to receiving the vacation you accrued but did not use.

As frustrating as the company was, you do not want to lose your vacation pay.

Also, you don't want to "burn bridges." Leaving immediately may lead to a bad reference, and it isn't worth that risk.

I have heard you should never burn your bridge. True or false? Have you done it?

It is true. All things considered, you should NOT burn a bridge. But, yes, I did burn a bridge once because of the way the organization treated me. It has never come back to haunt me in twenty-five years. However, I would not recommend it. In the scheme of things, it is not worth it.

FINAL THOUGHT:

Realize you can meet with all the right individuals and ask all the appropriate questions, and despite all this, there will be surprises. I hope they are not major. Just do your best to be prepared, and work hard.

F
My Résumé

THEODORE J. ZABORA

<u>Career Summary</u>

Six Sigma certified green belt and results oriented, senior human resources professional who has made a strategic impact on the organization. Have the skills and abilities to function effectively at the corporate or division level in diverse industries: manufacturing, research and development, service, advertising, banking, and healthcare.

Current Managerial Scope

Regional human resources responsibility for a $200M security company. Focus is aligning HR with the strategic direction of the organization as a member of the senior management team.

Major Experience Highlights

Compensation and Benefits:
- Designed and implemented long-term incentives, bonus plans, stock options, and perks for executives
- Developed and implemented an international and expatriate program
- Constructed incentive and bonus plans
- Implemented performance management programs
- Designed pay-for-performance programs
- Developed salary administration programs and salary structures
- Evaluated positions utilizing numerous types of job evaluation plans
- Significantly reduced benefit program costs ($1M)
- Managed all programs for 1,200 retirees; pension, medical and surviving spouse
- Implemented Board of Directors compensation plans
- Developed corporate philosophy and policy in the United States and Europe

Employee and Labor Relations:
- Focused proactively on employee relations
- Assured union avoidance by winning campaigns
- Developed programs, procedures, and policies for the United States and Europe
- Managed the significant downsizing and outplacement for eighty percent of an organization
- Managed a division closure after executive management decided it did not fit with the strategic direction of the corporation
- Directed contract negotiations as a member of the senior management team
- Managed grievance and arbitration proceedings
- Planned for a potential strike
- Improved union relations

Training and Development:
- Developed programs that led to cultural change
- Created a strategic training plan
- Integrated career development as a critical component of the performance management process
- Developed a succession plan

Recruitment:
- Recruited for all levels including executive management
- Conducted true executive searches

- Ramped up and recruited for a fifty percent increase in the workforce
- Successfully addressed severe labor shortages during a low employment period
- Developed and monitored measurement systems: cost per hire, length of time to fill positions, and sourcing effectiveness.

Human Resources Information Systems:
- Project manager for vendor and software selection including needs analysis, request for proposal (RFP) development, vendor evaluation, analysis, and complete implementation
- Experience with numerous integrated human resources and payroll systems

EEO/Affirmative Action:
- Resolved numerous discrimination complaints successfully
- Developed and implemented Affirmative Action Plans
- Managed fourteen OFCCP desk audits as well as a corporate management review (glass ceiling)

Major Accomplishments

- Published first book: *N-E-T-WORKING*
- Writing a manuscript for a second book
- Taught graduate-level human resource

management course for five years at Johns Hopkins University
- Annual guest lecturer at Western Maryland College (now McDaniel College)
- Contributed to "Best Places to Work" recognition of company (top fifty large companies in Pennsylvania). Recognized as a great place to work for living it's values, providing an excellent culture, and having a major HR focus
- Created new HR departments and HR functions on the corporate and division levels that contributed to the strategic direction of the organization
- Implemented Lean & Kan Ban, which enables a constant focus on improvements
- Successfully integrated five acquired companies
- Reduced benefit costs by thirty percent
- Established credible, responsive, and customer-focused functions in organizations experiencing significant growth and change
- Led and facilitated numerous efforts within a team structure
- Developed autonomous functions and strategic plans in order to sell a business
- Managed a complete division closure
- Established corporate philosophy and policies domestically and in Europe
- Presented regular updates to the company's Compensation Committee and Board of Directors
- Received Total Quality Management Award for

designing appraisal and pay training
- Led many non-HR projects such as a team which identified $2.9M in cost reductions (typically a finance initiative)

Education

B.S., Psychology—Towson University
M.A., Human Resources Management—Towson University

Professional Experience

Securitas Security Services USA, Frederick, Maryland
Vice President of Human Resources, Mid-Atlantic Region (April, 2006 – Present)

New Standard Corporation, York/Mount Joy, Pennsylvania
Director of Human Resources (2004–2006)

Vertis, Inc., Baltimore, Maryland
Corporate Director, Strategic Human Resources Initiatives (2003–2004)

Tate Access Floors, Inc., Jessup, Maryland/Red Lion, Pennsylvania
Director of Human Resources (1999–2003)

Provident Bank of Maryland, Baltimore, Maryland

Vice President of Executive Compensation and Employee Benefit Programs (1998–1999)

Applied Physics Laboratory, Laurel, Maryland
Manager, Human Resources (1993–1998)

Armco Stainless & Alloy Products, Baltimore, Maryland
Director, Compensation, Benefits, and HRIS (1990–1993)

Professional Recruiting/Executive
Search/Independent Contractor (1988–1990)

Equitable Bank, N.A., Baltimore, Maryland
Director of Human Resources/Corporate Director of Compensation (1986–1988)

PLEASE NOTE:

Because I worked for a number of companies which had significant US and foreign competition as well as other major challenges, I also developed a professional summary. It explains the specific reasons for each career change.

While I have received some negative feedback on my résumé over the years, I have also received the following: "Your résumé reflects an outstanding background. You are an excellent match." "We want to know more about your experience."

Remember, take the time to develop a well-written and organized résumé. It is the first impression the reader forms of you. Lastly, be receptive to constructive criticism and changes to your résumé. It will prove to be invaluable.

Index

Bibliography

Valvano, Jim. First Annual ESPY Awards, Acceptance Speech, March 4, 1993, http://www.jimmyv.org.

Acknowledgments

I could not have focused and written this book without the love and support from my best friend and wife, Nancy. A thank-you is insufficient to express my feelings. You are an incredible woman, wife, mother, and grandmother.

Brian and Craig, my sons, have made me extremely proud. They inspire and motivate me. I am an extremely lucky father.

To my daughter-in-law, Jenny. Thank you for your support and encouragement.

To Eric, my grandson. To my new grandson Gregory, who was born in October 2006. They always make us happy when we are sad or down and need a lift. Being a grandparent is one of life's incredible experiences. Is this a great life or what? WITHOUT QUESTION!

To my parents, Ted and Ceil Zabora. They communicated frequently the importance of a college education. While they have passed, this book is a testimony to their encouragement.

The Jesuits! What can I say? I never thought four years of Latin in high school would be a benefit in my life. However, it all comes around, and we finally understand and appreciate many things we learn in our younger years.

It is important to recognize my brother-in-law, Charlie. He always understood how organizations have impacted individuals who were laid off. He has been incredibly supportive and understanding over the last twenty-five years. Charlie, thank you.

To my professional and peer support system over several years. People like Katrina Smith, Larry Kuhn, Joy Biser, Gary Dupree, Wanda Rhinehart Felder, and Ann Miller. They supported and motivated me to focus on my nine-step process. Thank you from the bottom of my heart.

Jimmy Valvano coached the North Carolina State men's basketball team to a national championship. Coach V is so important to me for his encouragement to everyone: "DON'T GIVE UP. DON'T EVER GIVE UP!" It is so appropriate for this to be Step Nine in the networking process.

To the staff of American Book Business Press, who responded positively to my book proposal and made it a reality. Last, but not least, to Anna Brown, my editor, who helped me immensely to make the book the "best it could be." Anna, I thoroughly enjoyed our journey.

About the Author

Ted Zabora has worked in the human resources management field for thirty-five years. His educational background includes a bachelor's degree in psychology and a master's in HR management.

Ted is a certified Six Sigma green belt. His professional HR experience includes senior level, corporate, and division management positions both as a generalist and specialist in a wide variety of industries (R&D, manufacturing, marketing, banking, healthcare, and service).

He has aligned HR with the strategic business objectives of the organization. Ted's professional objective has been to make a significant impact and contribution.

His teaching experience includes five years at Johns Hopkins University. At JHU he taught a graduate level Human Resources Management course to technical students in the Whiting School of Engineering. Since 2000, he has been a regular guest lecturer at McDaniel College (formerly Western Maryland College) in their business and economics departments.

The McDaniel lectures are designed to provide the students with actual human resources case studies in order to give them the opportunity to learn from real life challenges and issues. There are theories and laws. Then there is real life.

The students discuss the pros and cons of each case. Ted concludes each discussion with the actual HR decision he or his team made, but more importantly, the reasons and rationale for the decision.

Ted and Nancy have been married for thirty-eight fantastic years. They have two sons, Brian and Craig, a daughter-in-law, Jenny, and two grandsons, Eric and Gregory. Life does not get any better than this.

Nancy retired after sixteen years as a nursery school director, administrator, and teacher. She is currently working part-time as the school's consultant and stays very busy helping the family with many activities like chasing and baby sitting Eric and Gregory.

Brian is a research analyst and has a B.B.A., MBA, and CFA. His recommendations and analyses play a major role in determining investment opportunities for their customers. He also enjoys participating in triathlons.

Craig is an account manager and graduated with a degree in Business and Economics in 2000. He played golf throughout high school and college. He and his teammates have had the thrill of winning conference championships as well as participating in the NCAA Division III Men's Championship.